Spain

Sue Townsend and Caroline Young

www.heinemann.co.uk/library
Visit our website to find out more information about **Heinemann Library** books.

To order:
 Phone 44 (0) 1865 888066
 Send a fax to 44 (0) 1865 314091
Visit the Heinemann Bookshop at www.heinemann.co.uk/library to browse our catalogue and order online.

First published in Great Britain by Heinemann Library, Halley Court, Jordan Hill, Oxford OX2 8EJ, part of Harcourt Education.

Heinemann is a registered trademark of Harcourt Education Ltd.

Editorial: Nancy Dickmann, Andrew Solway and Jennifer Tubbs
Design: Jo Hinton-Malivoire and Tinstar Design Limited (www.tinstar.co.uk)
Illustrations: Nicholas Beresford-Davies
Picture Research: Catherine Bevan
Production: Séverine Ribierre

Originated by Dot Gradations Ltd
Printed in China
by Wing King Tong

ISBN 0 431 11727 6
07 06 05 04 03
10 9 8 7 6 5 4 3 2 1

British Library Cataloguing in Publication Data
Townsend, Sue & Young, Caroline
Spain. – (A World of Recipes)
641.5'123'0946
A full catalogue record for this book is available from the British Library.

Acknowledgements
The publishers would like to thank the following for permission to reproduce photographs: Corbis: p. **5**; Gareth Boden: all other photographs.

Cover photographs reproduced with permission of Gareth Boden.

The publishers would like to thank Juan Sánchez for his assistance with the preparation of this book.

Every effort has been made to contact copyright holders of any material reproduced in this book. Any omissions will be rectified in subsequent printings if notice is given to the publishers.

Contents

Key

* easy

** medium

*** difficult

Words appearing in the text in bold, **like this**, are explained in the glossary.

Spanish food

Atlantic Ocean

Bay of Biscay

FRANCE

Bilbao

Barcelona

PORTUGAL

Madrid

Valencia

Balearic Islands

SPAIN

Granada

Mediterranean Sea

Strait of Gibraltar — Gibraltar (UK)

MOROCCO

ALGERIA

feet	HEIGHT	metres
over 13120		over 4000
6560–13120		2000–4000
3277–6557		1000–1999
1640–3277		500–999
656–1637		200–499
under 656		under 200

kilometres 0   100   200
miles 0   50   100   150

Spain is famous for its sunny climate and its beaches, but most of the country is very mountainous. In the north, the Pyrenees mountains divide Spain from France. Much of the land is covered by the *meseta*, (pronounced *meh-SEH-ta*), which means 'table-land'. This is a huge platform, criss-crossed by mountain ranges, and home to bears, lynxes and eagles. The capital city, Madrid, is the highest capital in Europe.

In the past

Many peoples have ruled Spain over the centuries, each with their own customs and cooking styles. People who lived there more than 15,000 years ago left spectacular paintings on the cave walls in Altamira, in northern Spain. Then followed invasions by people from north Africa and Greece, and Celts from north of the Pyrenees. The country was ruled by the Roman Empire for 400 years, and then followed centuries of rule by people from the Muslim faith, called Moors. In 1492, the states of Spain were united under the rule of the Christian King Ferdinand and Queen Isabella. The Spanish Empire grew, based on riches sent back from the New World by explorers called **conquistadors**. Spanish people used the new foods they brought back, such as peppers and potatoes, in their cookery – and they still do today.

▲ *A fruit and vegetable stall at Boqueria Market in Barcelona, Spain.*

Around the country

Farming in Spain is mainly based around the coasts, where the land is most **fertile**. Spanish farmers grow grains, tomatoes, oranges, lemons, vegetables, almonds, olives and strong onions, **exporting** them to many other countries. Some wines come from the northern area, around La Rioja. Perhaps Spain's most plentiful crop is fish, because the waters around Spain are full of fish and shellfish.

Spanish meals

So many different peoples have lived in Spain during its history that there are many cooking styles, or *cocinas*. People may visit a **tapas** bar, which serves a selection of tasty dishes, to eat. An afternoon nap, called a *siesta*, might be followed by a snack called *merienda* – perhaps a hot chocolate and a cake. Evening meals often have many dishes and are enjoyed by the whole family.

Ingredients

tomatoes

courgette

olive oil

peppers

asparagus

orange

onion

olives

almonds

Serrano ham

blanched almonds

cinnamon stick

saffron

chorizo

Almonds

In Spain, almonds are used to flavour cakes, biscuits and sweets. Most supermarkets sell almonds blanched (with the shell and bitter brown skin removed), **flaked**, **ground** or **chopped**.

Chorizo

These spicy pork sausages come already cooked or cured. They are sliced and chopped, and added to savoury dishes for flavour. Chorizos may have slightly different ingredients in different parts of Spain.

Olive oil

Spanish cooks **fry** food and make **dressings** for salads in oil made from olives. Fresh olives are also served as a snack.

Onions

Many farmers grow onions in Spain. Spanish onions have a stronger, slightly less sweet flavour than other onions. You can use them to make the recipes in this book, if you like.

Oranges

Oranges are a very important crop in Spain. Some are bitter, and are used to make marmalade. They are called Seville oranges, because they grow around the southern city of Seville. Sweeter types grow around the city of Valencia, in the south-east. They are delicious eaten fresh, in desserts, or made into juice.

Peppers

When red, yellow or orange peppers are cooked, they develop a sweet, smoky taste. Green peppers are unripe red peppers, and have a slightly bitter flavour. Most supermarkets sell fresh peppers.

Saffron

The yellow threads (or stigma) found in the centre of crocus flowers are called saffron. Saffron is very expensive because it takes so long to harvest. It adds a golden yellow colour and a honey-like flavour to food. You can buy it in small packets in most supermarkets.

Serrano ham

Traditionally, this ham comes from the mountainous area of north-east Spain. *Serrano* means 'from the mountains' in Spanish. If you cannot find it, you can use another dry, **cured** ham instead, such as Parma ham, which most supermarkets sell.

Before you start

Kitchen rules

There are a few basic rules you should always follow when you are cooking:

- Ask an adult if you can use the kitchen.
- Some cooking processes, especially those involving hot water or oil, can be dangerous. When you see this sign, take extra care or ask an adult to help.
- Wash your hands before you start.
- Wear an apron to protect your clothes.
- Be very careful when you use sharp knives.
- Never leave pan handles sticking out, in case you knock them.
- Use oven gloves to lift things in and out of the oven.
- Wash fruits and vegetables before you use them.
- Always wash chopping boards very well after use, especially after chopping raw meat, fish or poultry.
- Use a separate chopping board for onions and garlic, if possible.

How long will it take?

Some of the recipes in this book are quick and easy, and some are more difficult and take longer. The strip across the right-hand side of each recipe page tells you how long it takes to prepare a dish from start to finish. It also shows how difficult it is to make – each recipe is * (easy), ** (medium) or *** (difficult).

Quantities and measurements

You can see how many people each recipe will serve at the top of each right-hand page. You can multiply or divide the quantities if you want to cook for more or fewer people.

Ingredients for recipes can be measured in two different ways. Metric measurements use grams and millilitres. Imperial measurements use ounces and fluid ounces. This book uses metric measurements. If you want to convert these into imperial measurements, see the chart on page 44.

In the recipes, you will see the following abbreviations:

tbsp = tablespoon   g = grams
tsp = teaspoon   ml = millilitres

Utensils

To cook the recipes in this book, you will need these utensils (as well as essentials, such as spoons, plates and bowls):

- plastic or glass chopping board (easier to clean than wooden ones)
- blender or food processor
- large frying pan
- large, high-sided frying pan with lid
- 18 cm heavy-based non-stick frying pan
- small and large saucepans with lids
- measuring jug
- sieve
- set of scales
- sharp knife
- baking sheets
- balloon whisk
- pastry brush
- tongs
- paper cake cases.

 Whenever you use kitchen knives, be very careful.

Gazpacho (Cold tomato soup)

This dish is traditionally from southern Spain, where summers are very hot. Serve it in a bowl as a starter, or in a glass as a cool drink.

What you need

1 red pepper
700 g tomatoes
half a cucumber
1 small onion
1 clove garlic
1 tbsp fresh parsley
1 tbsp white wine vinegar
2 tbsp olive oil
50 g fresh breadcrumbs
1 slice bread

What you do

1 Cut the pepper in half, then cut each half into three strips. Throw away the seeds and stalk.

(!) **2** Lay the pepper skin side up on a grill. **Grill** for 5 minutes, until the skin blackens. Put it into a plastic box and **cover** it.

3 When cool, **peel** off the pepper's skin.

(!) **4** Put the tomatoes into a colander in a large bowl in the sink. Pour in just-boiled water and leave for 1 minute.

5 Lift the colander out. Cut a cross on the bottom of each tomato and peel off the skin.

6 Cut the tomatoes in half. Scoop the seeds into a sieve over a bowl.

7 Put the tomatoes and pepper into a blender. Add any juice from the tomato seeds.

8 Peel the cucumber, cut off a 2 cm piece and put it aside. **Chop** the rest and add it to the blender.

9 Peel and finely chop the onion and garlic. Chop the parsley. Add them to the blender with the white wine vinegar, oil and breadcrumbs. **Blend** until smooth.

10 Add salt and pepper to taste. If your soup is too thick, add a little cold water. **Chill** for 2 hours.

11 Cut the crusts off the bread. Cut the bread and the leftover piece of cucumber into 1 cm cubes.

12 Serve in bowls **garnished** with bread cubes and cucumber.

Asparagus with ham

In northern Spain, farmers sell their crops of green and white asparagus in local markets each spring. This delicately flavoured vegetable is often made into **tapas** (see box on page 17). It makes an ideal snack or light lunch.

What you need

12 asparagus spears
6 slices dry, **cured** ham (Serrano ham, if available)
1 tbsp olive oil
freshly **ground** black pepper

What you do

1 Trim any hard, woody bits off the bottom of the asparagus stems.

2 Holding the asparagus in a bundle with the tips facing the same way, tap the bottoms on a board to make them level.

3 Wrap a piece of foil around the top of the asparagus. It should come two-thirds of the way down the stems.

4 Pour water into a saucepan until it is 4 cm deep. Stand the asparagus up in the water with the tips upwards. **Cover** and bring to the **boil**, and boil for 3 minutes.

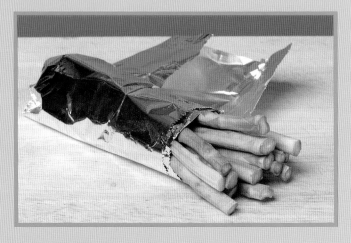

5 Using a slotted spoon, lift the asparagus into a bowl of cold water. Take the foil off.

6 Cut the slices of ham in half lengthways. Wrap a slice around each asparagus spear.

(!) 7 **Preheat** a medium hot grill. Brush the ham with olive oil and **grill** for 3 minutes on each side.

8 Serve hot, sprinkled with freshly-ground black pepper.

SIESTAS

Summer afternoons are so hot in Spain that some people take a nap, called a *siesta*. Shops and cafes close, opening again in the early evening, when it is cooler.

Prawns in batter

Spanish markets and supermarkets are full of the many different kinds of fish and shellfish caught off the coasts of Spain. This dish uses large prawns, and can be served as a **tapa** (see box on page 17) or as a starter. If you are using frozen prawns, you need to **defrost** them first.

What you need

½ tsp saffron strands
(about 8)
50 g plain flour
pinch of salt
100 ml sparkling
mineral water
20 large prawns, **peeled**
but not cooked
4 tbsp olive oil

To garnish:
sprigs of fresh flat leaf
parsley

What you do

1 Put the saffron into 1 tbsp hot water to soak.

2 Meanwhile, **sift** the flour into a bowl. Add a pinch of salt.

3 Stir in a quarter of the sparkling water to make a smooth, thick batter. Add the rest of the water a little at a time, stirring well.

4 Stir the saffron mixture. Crush the strands with a teaspoon to release the colour.

5 Put a sieve over a bowl and pour the yellow liquid through it. Stir the liquid into the batter.

6 Lay the prawns on to kitchen paper, and pat them dry. (They need to be dry for the batter to **coat** them properly.)

7 Heat the oil in a frying pan. Spear each prawn with a fork or a wooden **skewer**, and dip it into the batter. Put the prawn into the pan and **fry** for 2–3 minutes, turning it over half way through the cooking time. Fry a few prawns at a time.

8 Lift the cooked prawns onto kitchen paper to **drain**.

9 Serve the prawns garnished with sprigs of parsley.

Spicy potatoes

This dish, called *patatas bravas* in Spanish, is very popular as a lunchtime snack. The potatoes are flavoured with a tangy red spice called paprika, which is made from dried red peppers grown in central-west Spain. Medium-sized new potatoes are the best ones to use.

What you need

550 g potatoes
1 tbsp olive oil
1 tbsp paprika
1 tsp ground cumin
½ tsp chilli powder
(if you like it)

To **garnish***:*
sprigs of fresh flat
    leaf parsley

What you do

1 **Preheat** the oven to gas mark 5/190 °C/375 °F.

2 Wash and **peel** the potatoes. Cut them into 2 cm chunks.

(!) 3 Put the potato chunks into a pan, add a pinch of salt and cover them with hot water. Bring the water to the **boil**, and boil for 3 minutes.

4 Carefully **drain** the potatoes and put them into a bowl.

5 Add the oil, paprika, cumin, chilli powder and a pinch of salt to the potatoes. Gently stir the potatoes so that you **coat** them with the spices but do not break the chunks. Spoon the potatoes into a roasting tin.

6 Cook the potatoes in the oven for 20 minutes, or until they feel soft when you stick the end of a knife into them.

7 Spoon the potatoes into a serving dish. Serve hot or cold, garnished with parsley.

TAPAS BARS

In Spain, tapas bars serve a wide choice of different tapas dishes, usually served in small portions. People can choose just one dish to have with a beer or coffee, a few to eat as a light lunch, or they can share a larger selection of tapas with friends.

17

Courgette and aubergine fritters

Spanish farmers **export** many different vegetables to other countries. This dish is from the Balearic Islands of Ibiza, Majorca and Menorca, a Spanish province. It is ideal as a **tapa** (see box on page 17), or as a side dish. Spanish cooks may dip the yellow flowers of the courgette plant in batter and cook them as well.

What you need

50 g plain flour
pinch of salt
1 egg
80 ml milk
2 courgettes
1 aubergine
4 tbsp olive oil

What you do

1 **Sift** the flour and a pinch of salt into a bowl.

2 Lightly **beat** the egg with a fork. Stir in the milk.

3 Add the milk mixture to the flour. **Whisk** well with a balloon whisk to make a smooth batter.

4 Trim both ends off the courgettes and aubergine. **Slice** the courgette into 1 cm slices.

5 Cut the aubergine into 1 cm slices. If the aubergine is large, cut the slices in half again.

6 **Preheat** the oven to gas mark 3/170 °C/325 °F.

(!) 7 Heat half the oil in a frying pan over a medium heat. Using a fork, dip a vegetable slice into the batter. Let the excess batter drip off before putting the vegetable slice into the frying pan.

8 **Fry** for 2 minutes on each side, until the slices are golden brown. You can cook several slices at the same time.

9 Put kitchen paper on to a baking sheet. Lift each slice on to the baking sheet, and keep warm in the oven while you fry the rest.

10 Serve hot, sprinkled with salt and pepper.

Paella (Rice with chicken and prawns)

Paella is probably Spain's most famous dish. It is not easy to make, so you will need adult help. In Spain, what goes into a paella varies according to what is available, or traditional, in different areas. Paella recipes can be passed down through generations of a family. Try this version, then experiment.

What you need

225 g fresh mussels (cook them on the day you buy them)
2 chicken stock cubes
½ tsp saffron strands
2 tbsp olive oil
4 chicken leg portions, cut in half
1 large onion
2 cloves garlic
225 g paella rice or short grain rice
4 tomatoes
100 g chorizo sausages
150 g frozen peas
175 g **peeled** prawns, **defrosted** if frozen

To garnish:
lemon wedges

What you do

1 Put the mussels into clean water. Scrub each one, pulling off any feathery bits. Throw away any that have cracked or slightly-open shells.

(!) 2 Fill a pan with **boiling** water and add the mussels. **Cover** and cook over a high heat for 5 minutes.

(!) 3 Tip the mussels into a colander. Throw away any that have closed shells.

4 Crumble the stock cubes into 825 ml of hot water. Stir in the saffron.

(!) 5 Heat the oil in a large, high-sided non-stick frying pan over a medium to high heat. **Fry** the chicken pieces for 4–5 minutes on each side.

6 Cover the pan and cook the chicken over a medium heat for 10 minutes. Carefully lift the chicken onto a plate.

7 Peel and **chop** the onion and garlic finely. Put them and the rice into the pan. **Stir-fry** for 3 minutes, until the rice becomes see-through.

(!) 8 Stir in a quarter of the stock. Bring to the boil, add the chicken and the rest of the stock, and boil again. Cover and **simmer** for 10 minutes, stirring occasionally.

9 Cut the tomatoes into quarters. Cut the chorizo into 1 cm chunks or **slices**.

10 Stir the tomatoes, chorizo, peas, prawns and mussels into the pan. Add a little more hot water if needed. Cover and simmer for 10 minutes.

11 Spoon the paella into a serving dish. Garnish with lemon wedges and serve.

Pork fillet with almonds

This recipe is from Jerez in south-west Spain, an area famous for producing a strong, sweet wine called sherry. Serve it as a main dish, with potatoes or rice and a selection of vegetables.

What you need

50 g blanched almonds
900 g pork fillet
1 onion
2 tbsp olive oil
1 tbsp sherry vinegar or white wine vinegar
1 pork or vegetable stock cube
2 tsp cornflour
142 ml pot single cream

*To **garnish:***
sprigs of fresh parsley

What you do

(!) 1 Dry-fry the almonds until they are lightly browned. Tip them onto a plate.

2 Lay the pork fillet on a board. Without cutting through to the board, cut a slit from one end to the other. (If the fillet is in two pieces, cut a slit in each.)

3 Scatter the almonds over the pork and bring the two edges together. Knot the fillet together with string, making each knot about 5 cm apart.

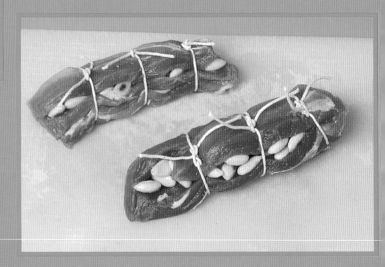

4 Peel and **chop** the onion.

(!) 5 Heat the oil in a deep frying pan. Add the fillet and **fry** for 2–3 minutes on each side, until it is lightly browned.

6 Add the onion and fry over a medium heat for 3 minutes.

7 Put the sherry vinegar and 300 ml hot water into a measuring jug. Crumble the stock cube into the liquid and stir well.

8 Add the liquid to the pan, bring to the **boil**, **cover** and **simmer** for 1 hour.

9 Carefully lift the meat out of the pan and snip off the string. Cut the meat into thick **slices** and arrange on a plate.

10 Stir the cornflour and cream together in a jug. Add the cooking juices from the meat.

11 Pour the mixture back into the pan. **Reheat** for 2 minutes, stirring all the time. Pour over the pork and serve, garnished with parsley.

Potato and onion omelette

In Spain, this vegetable omelette is called a *tortilla* (pronounced *Tor-TEE-ya*). Spanish people serve it hot or cold in wedges, as a snack or part of a picnic. It makes a perfect snack or light lunch.

What you need

75 g potatoes
1 onion
4 eggs
1 tbsp olive oil

To garnish:
1 tomato

What you do

1 Wash and **peel** the potatoes.

2 Cut a 1 cm **slice** off the side of each potato and stand it flat on a board. Cut it into 1 cm wide slices, and then chop it into cubes.

3 Peel and slice the onion thinly.

4 Crack the eggs into a bowl. Add 2 tbsp cold water, and some salt and pepper. **Beat** them lightly with a fork.

(!) 5 Heat the oil in a large non-stick frying pan. Add the potato and **fry** over a low-medium heat for 4 minutes, or until potato is soft.

6 Add the onion and cook for 10 minutes, stirring sometimes. **Preheat** a grill to medium.

7 Turn the heat up a little under the frying pan. Pour the beaten eggs over the potato and onion mixture and cook for 4–5 minutes.

8 Put the pan under the grill, but keep the handle out. Cook until the egg has set, and is starting to brown.

9 Slide a fish slice around the edges of the tortilla. Hold the pan just above one side of a dinner plate, and slide the tortilla on to the plate.

10 Cut the tomato into wedges. Cut the tortilla into wedges, and serve hot or cold, garnished with the tomato.

SPANISH OMELETTE

When cooks add potatoes, onions, peas, slices of pepper, green beans, asparagus, mushrooms or ham to an omelette, they are making a dish known in many countries as a Spanish omelette. It is an ideal way to use up leftover vegetables.

Roast d vegetabl salad

In Spain, people eat this salad as a main dish, using chunks of crusty bread as a scoop, instead of knives and forks. It makes an ideal starter or side dish, too.

What you need

1 onion
1 green pepper
1 yellow pepper
1 red pepper
2 tbsp olive oil for
   brushing peppers

For the garlic dressing:
4 cloves garlic
½ tsp **ground** cumin
4 tbsp olive oil
1 lemon

What you do

1 **Preheat** the oven to gas mark 5/190 °C/375 °F.

2 Wrap the onion in foil, put it on to a baking sheet and **bake** for 15 minutes.

3 Brush the peppers with oil.

(!) 4 Arrange the peppers and garlic around the onion. Put back in the oven for 20 minutes. Put the hot peppers into a plastic box and cover them.

5 When it is cool, take the foil off the onion, **peel** off its skin and cut the flesh into thin strips.

6 Peel the skin off the peppers. Cut them in half, then into thin strips, throwing away the seeds and stalk. Arrange them on a plate.

7 Cut the end off each clove of garlic. Squeeze the flesh inside into a small bowl and squash it with a teaspoon to make a paste.

8 Cut the lemon in half. Use a lemon squeezer to squeeze out the juice.

9 Add the cumin, 4 tbsp oil, lemon juice and salt and pepper to the garlic paste.

10 Spoon the garlic dressing over the vegetables and serve.

Haricot bean and pork stew

Traditionally, miners working deep inside the mountains of northern Spain ate this filling stew, which is called *fabada*. Spanish cooks add a piece of black pudding, but this recipe uses pork sausages.

What you need

350 g dried haricot beans
450 g piece smoked
  gammon
100 g belly pork
  (optional)
200 g pork sausages
200 g chorizo sausages
3 saffron strands
freshly-**ground**
  black pepper

What you do

1 Put the beans and the gammon into separate large bowls. Cover both with 2 litres of cold water. Leave them in the fridge overnight.

2 If using belly pork, cut off the dark rind.

(!) 3 **Drain** the beans into a colander and put them into a large saucepan. Add the belly pork, sausages, chorizo and gammon. Cover with cold water. Bring to the **boil**, and boil for 10 minutes.

(!) 4 Using a slotted spoon, carefully skim any white froth off the boiling liquid.

5 Add the saffron, **cover** and **simmer** for 1½ hours, stirring occasionally. Add more water to keep the beans covered if you need to.

(!) 6 Take the pan off the heat. Using a slotted spoon, lift the pieces of meat on to a chopping board. Cut them into bite-sized pieces.

7 Put the meat back into the pan and **reheat** thoroughly.

8 Add some freshly-ground black pepper, and serve in bowls with crusty bread.

Cod croquettes

Croquettes are a popular **tapa** (see box on page 17), or side dish, all over Spain. They are made by mixing mashed potato or thick white sauce with fish, ham or cheese, and rolling them into a sausage shape. Then they are **coated** in breadcrumbs and fried.

What you need

450 g cod fillet
 (or any white fish)
450 ml milk
1 onion
5 tbsp olive oil
5 tbsp cornflour
ground black pepper
1 tbsp fresh dill
1 tbsp plain flour
2 eggs
150 g white
  breadcrumbs

To garnish:
sprigs of fresh dill
wedges of lemon

What you do

(!) 1 Put the fish into a saucepan. Add the milk, **cover** and bring to the **boil**.

2 **Simmer** for 3 minutes, then leave to cool.

3 Using a fish slice, lift the fish onto a plate. **Flake** it with a fork, throwing away any skin or bones.

4 Pour the cooking liquid into a measuring jug. Add cold water to make it up to 480 ml.

5 **Peel** the onion and **chop** it finely.

(!) 6 Heat 1 tbsp of the oil in the saucepan and **fry** the onion over a medium heat for 3 minutes.

7 In a bowl, stir 6 tbsp of the cooking liquid into the cornflour to make a smooth paste.

8 Stir in the rest of the cooking liquid. Pour it over the onions and cook, stirring all the time, until the liquid thickens.

9 Chop the dill finely. Add it to the onions with the fish and some black pepper. Leave to cool for 1 hour. **Chill** for at least 2 hours.

10 Sprinkle flour over a work surface. Roll 3 tbsp of the chilled mixture into a sausage shape 8–10 cm long. Repeat until you have used all the mixture.

11 **Beat** the eggs and pour them into a shallow bowl. Put the breadcrumbs on to a plate.

12 Dip the sausage shapes into the egg, and then roll them in the breadcrumbs.

① 13 Heat the rest of the oil in a frying pan over a medium heat. Fry the croquettes for 5 minutes, turning occasionally.

14 Serve garnished with sprigs of dill and lemon wedges.

Artichokes with garlic mayonnaise

Artichokes, known as *alcachofas* in Spanish, were first introduced to Spain by the Moors (see page 5). They are only available in Spain for a short period each year. To eat them Spanish-style, peel off a leaf, dip it into the garlic mayonnaise and scrape the flesh off with your teeth.

What you need

4 globe artichokes
pinch of salt
2 tbsp lemon juice

For the garlic mayonnaise:
16 tbsp ready-made
  mayonnaise
4 cloves of garlic

What you do

1 Twist or cut the stalks off the artichokes. Snip the pointed ends off the leaves with scissors.

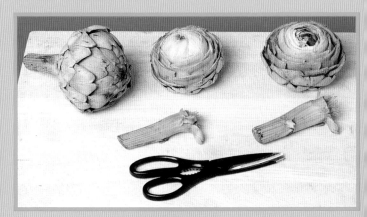

2 Put the artichokes into cold water with a pinch of salt.

3 Cut a lemon in half and squeeze out the juice with a lemon squeezer.

(!) 4 Bring a large pan of water to the **boil**. Add 2 tbsp of the lemon juice.

(!) 5 Using a slotted spoon, lower the artichokes into the pan, one at a time.

6 Bring back to the boil. **Cover** and **simmer** for 40 minutes.

7 Peel and crush the garlic. Stir it into the mayonnaise.

(!) 8 Lift the artichokes out of the pan with a slotted spoon. **Drain** them upside down in a colander until cool enough to handle.

9 Twist off the leaves in the middle of each artichoke. Scoop out the hairy bits in the centre with a teaspoon.

10 Put the leaves you took from the middle back into each artichoke, and serve warm or cold with the garlic mayonnaise.

33

Red pepper salad

This dish is known as *Ensalada de pimientos asados* in Spanish. It a speciality of the Rioja region of northern Spain, which is famous for its red wines. When the farmers prune the vines after the grape harvest, they pile the twigs into big bonfires. Traditionally, local people roast peppers in the hot embers and make them into salads like this one.

What you need

4 red peppers
2 yellow peppers
2 cloves garlic
1 large beefsteak tomato
   or 3 medium tomatoes
3 tbsp olive oil
2 tsp sherry vinegar or
   white wine vinegar

What you do

1 **Preheat** the oven to gas mark 5/190 °C/375 °F.

2 Put the peppers, garlic and tomato (or tomatoes) on a baking tray in the oven for 10 minutes.

3 Take the garlic and tomato (or tomatoes) off the tray, and leave the peppers to cook for an extra 10 minutes.

4 Cut the tomato (or tomatoes) into several pieces, and put them into a large sieve. Using the back of a spoon, push the tomato flesh and juice through the sieve. Throw away the skin and seeds.

5 Cut the end off the garlic and squeeze out the soft flesh. Stir into the tomato mixture.

6 Put the peppers into a plastic box with the lid on. Leave them to cool.

7 **Peel** the skin from the peppers and cut them in half. Cut off the stalks and scoop out the seeds, and throw the stalks and seeds away.

8 Cut the peppers into thin strips and arrange them on a plate.

9 Stir the oil and vinegar, and some salt and pepper, into the tomato mixture.

10 Spoon over the peppers and serve.

Nut sweets

These soft sweets are called *turron* (pronounced *tu-RON*) in Spain. This *turron* recipe was first made in a village called Jijona in Alicante, a part of Spain famous for its almond trees.

What you need

1 sheet rice paper
100 g blanched almonds
75 g blanched hazelnuts
2 egg whites
75 g caster sugar
4 tbsp set honey
1 tsp ground cinnamon

What you do

1 Cover a baking tray with a sheet of rice paper.

2 **Dry-fry** the almonds and hazelnuts in a frying pan until pale brown. Tip them on to a plate to cool.

3 Put the almonds and hazelnuts into a blender. **Blend** until they are finely **ground**.

4 To separate the egg yolks from the whites, carefully crack the egg. Keeping the yolk in one half of the shell, let the white drip into a bowl. Pass the yolk from one half of the shell to the other until all the white has dripped out. Put the yolk in a separate bowl. Do this for both eggs. (If there is any yolk in the white, crack another egg and try again.)

5 Using an electric whisk, **whisk** the egg whites until they are frothy and firm.

6 **Fold** in the nuts with a metal spoon.

(!) 7 Put the sugar and honey into a non-stick saucepan. Heat them gently until the sugar **dissolves**. Bring the liquid to the **boil** and add the nut mixture.

8 Cook over a low heat for 5 minutes, stirring all the time.

9 Spoon on to the rice paper and shape into a square about 2 cm deep and 24 cm wide. Leave to cool.

10 Lift the *turron* on to a board. Sprinkle it with cinnamon, and cut it into 2 cm squares, ready to eat.

Torrijas (Sugary egg-fried bread)

Torrijas (pronounced *tor-EE-has*) are a tea-time favourite in Spain. They are simple to make and an ideal way of using up stale bread. Serve with a bowl of milk to dip the *torrijas* into, if you want to be really traditional.

What you need

250 ml milk
½ tsp **ground** cinnamon
3 tbsp caster sugar
8 slices of baguette, 2 cm thick
2 eggs
2 tbsp olive oil
extra ½ tsp ground cinnamon

What you do

(!) **1** Put the milk, cinnamon and 2 tbsp of the caster sugar into a small saucepan. Bring to the **boil**. Turn off the heat and leave to cool for 5 minutes.

2 Arrange the bread slices in a shallow dish.

3 Pour the milk over the bread and leave for 10 minutes.

4 Lightly **beat** the eggs. Pour them into a shallow bowl.

5 Dip the bread slices into the beaten eggs to **coat** both sides.

(!) **6** Heat 1 tbsp of the oil in a frying pan until it is hot, but not smoking. Using a fish slice, lift two or three bread slices into the pan.

7 **Fry** over a medium to low heat for 2 minutes, until the underside is starting to brown. Use the fish slice to turn the bread over, and cook the other side.

8 Put the cooked bread slices on to a wire rack. Add the rest of the oil to the pan and cook the rest of the bread slices.

9 Mix 1 tbsp caster sugar and the extra cinnamon together. Sprinkle them over the warm bread and serve straightaway.

Magdalenas (Olive oil cakes)

For hundreds of years, the Spanish ate *magdalenas* (pronounced *mag-da-LAY-nas*) only on special holidays. Today, they eat them every day, at breakfast and tea-time. Traditionally, cooks add olive oil to the recipe, and **bake** each little cake in a specially shaped tin. However, you can make them just as well in paper cake cases.

What you need

125 g self raising flour
50 g caster sugar
1 lemon
100 ml olive oil
1 tbsp milk
3 eggs
1 tsp icing sugar

What you do

1 **Preheat** the oven to gas mark 5/190 °C/375 °F.

2 Put paper cases into a tin for making 12 small cakes.

3 **Sift** the flour and sugar into a bowl.

4 **Grate** the lemon over a plate, using the fine side of the grater. Add the grated lemon rind to the flour and sugar.

5 Measure the oil into a measuring jug, and add the milk.

6 To separate the egg yolks from the whites, carefully crack the egg. Keeping the yolk in one half of the shell, let the white drip into a bowl. Pass the yolk from one half of the shell to the other until all the white has dripped out. Add the yolk to the oil and milk. Do this for both eggs. (If there is any yolk in the white, crack another egg and try again.)

7 Use an electric whisk to **whisk** the egg whites until they are frothy and firm.

8 Mix the oil, milk and egg yolk mixture into the flour. Add half of the egg whites. Gently **fold** them into the flour mixture using a large metal spoon. Fold in the rest of the egg whites.

9 Spoon the mixture into the paper cases. **Bake** for 8–10 minutes, until the cakes are risen and golden.

10 Cool on a wire rack. **Dust** with icing sugar (see page 43) and serve.

Walnut puffs

These puff-pastry squares are a popular Christmas treat in the Asturias region of northern Spain. Many farmhouses there have walnut trees in their gardens, and people use the nuts in their cooking.

What you need

2 tsp plain flour
175 g packet ready-made puff pastry
40 g walnut pieces
1 tbsp icing sugar
1 tbsp honey
1 egg
1 tsp icing sugar

What you do

1 Sprinkle the flour over a work surface. Roll the pastry into a square about 24 cm wide with a rolling pin. Trim off any rough edges.

2 Cut the pastry into four strips, each 6 cm wide. Cut these in half to make eight rectangles 6 cm wide and 12 cm long.

3 **Chill** the pastry in the fridge.

4 Meanwhile, **blend** the walnut pieces in a blender until finely **chopped**.

5 Put the nuts, icing sugar and honey into a bowl, and stir well.

6 **Preheat** the oven to gas mark 7/210 °C/425 °F. Brush the edges of the pastry with a little water.

7 Put 1 tsp of the walnut mixture at one end of each pastry rectangle, leaving a rim of pastry around the edge.

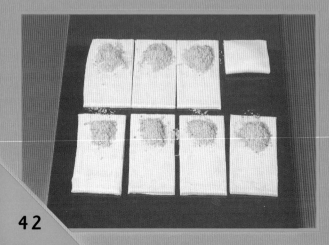

8 Fold the pastry over to make a square.

9 Press down the edges with the back of a fork. Put the squares onto a baking tray.

10 **Beat** the egg in a bowl with a fork. Brush some over the pastry.

(!) **11** **Bake** the puffs on the top shelf of the oven for 8–10 minutes, until golden. Lift on to a wire rack to cool.

12 **Dust** with icing sugar (see below). Serve warm or cold.

DUSTING

To add the finishing touch to cakes, spoon 1 tsp of icing sugar into a sieve. Hold the sieve over the cake and lightly tap the side with the spoon. This is called dusting.

Further information

Here are some places to find out more about Spain and Spanish cooking.

Books

Getting to Know Spain and Spanish, Janet De Saulles (Barrons Education Series, 1993)
Spain: Picture a Country, Henry Pluckrose (Franklin Watts, 1999)
Spanish Cooking, Pepita Aris (Apple Press, 2000)
The Book of Tapas and Spanish Cooking, Hilaire Walden (Salamander Books, 1998)

Websites

www.spanish-kitchen.co.uk
www.bbc.co.uk/education/languages/spanish
www.lingolex.com/spanishfood/recipes/htm

Conversion chart

Ingredients for recipes can be measured in two different ways. Metric measurements use grams and millilitres. Imperial measurements use ounces and fluid ounces. This book uses metric measurements. The chart here shows you how to convert measurements from metric to imperial.

SOLIDS		LIQUIDS	
METRIC	IMPERIAL	METRIC	IMPERIAL
10 g	¼ oz	30 ml	1 fl oz
15 g	½ oz	50 ml	2 fl oz
25 g	1 oz	75 ml	2½ fl oz
50 g	1¾ oz	100 ml	3½ fl oz
75 g	2¾ oz	125 ml	4 fl oz
100 g	3½ oz	150 ml	5 fl oz
150 g	5 oz	300 ml	10 fl oz
250 g	9 oz	600 ml	20 fl oz
450 g	16 oz		

Healthy eating

This diagram shows which foods you should eat to stay healthy. Most of your food should come from the bottom of the food pyramid. Eat some of the foods from the middle every day. Only eat a little of the foods from the top.

Healthy eating, Spanish-style

Spanish food varies a great deal. Some dishes are served with rice, others with potatoes or bread. Many recipes use a lot of vegetables from the middle layer of this pyramid, cooking them without much fat or oil. The Spanish eat a lot of fruit and fish, because both are plentiful. People in Spain enjoy cakes, but they tend to be small, eaten as a taste of something sweet after a main meal.

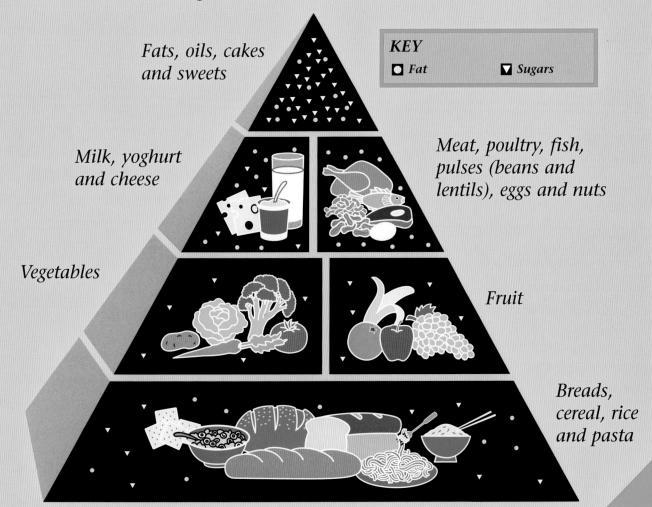

Fats, oils, cakes and sweets

KEY
◻ *Fat*   ▽ *Sugars*

Milk, yoghurt and cheese

Meat, poultry, fish, pulses (beans and lentils), eggs and nuts

Vegetables

Fruit

Breads, cereal, rice and pasta

Glossary

bake cook something in the oven

beat mix ingredients together strongly, using a fork or whisk

blend mix ingredients together in an electric blender or food processor

boil cook a liquid on the hob. Boiling liquid bubbles and steams strongly.

chill put a dish in the fridge for a while to cool down

chop cut into pieces using a sharp knife

coat cover with a mixture or sauce

conquistadors explorers sent from Spain to find and conquer new lands

cover put a lid on a pan, or put foil or cling film over a dish

cured food, usually cooked meat, that is specially dried and flavoured

defrost allow something that is frozen to thaw, that is, to get warmer so that the ice melts. This should be done in the fridge.

dissolve mix something, such as sugar, until it disappears into a liquid

drain remove liquid, usually by pouring something into a colander or sieve

dressing sauce for a salad

dry-fry cook over a high heat without any oil

dust sprinkle with icing sugar or flour

export sell something, such as oranges, to another country

fertile with rich soil, which produces excellent crops

flake break into flakes

fold mixing wet and dry ingredients by making cutting movements with a metal spoon

fry cook something in oil in a pan

garnish decorate food, for example, with fresh herbs

grate break something, such as cheese, into small pieces using a grater

grill cook under a grill

ground made into a fine powder

peel remove the skin of a fruit or vegetable

preheat warm up the oven in advance

reheat heat food thoroughly again

sift remove lumps from dry ingredients, such as flour, with a sieve

simmer cook liquid on the hob. Simmering liquid bubbles and steams gently.

skewer long wooden stick for holding food

slice cut something into thin, flat pieces

stir-fry cook foods in a little oil over a high heat, stirring all the time

tapa small dish of Spanish food, often served with a selection of others

thaw see defrost

whisk mix ingredients together using a whisk

Index

Titles in the A World of Recipes series include:

Hardback   0431 117268

Hardback   0431 11725X

Hardback   0431 117284

Hardback   0431 117276

Hardback   0431 117306

Hardback   0431 117292

Find out about the other titles in this series on our website www.heinemann.co.uk/library